Leigh Lawson was born in 1943 in Warwickshire and trained at Mountview Academy and the Royal Academy of Dramatic Art in London.

He has played leading roles at The Royal Shakespeare Company, The National Theatre, in the West End, and on Broadway. In the theatre he has worked with directors including Peter Hall, Peter Gill, Adrian Noble, Michael Rudman, and Sean Mathias. He has played principal roles in over 20 feature films, including *Brother Sun, Sister Moon* (dir. Franco Zeffirelli), *Love Among the Ruins* (dir. George Cukor), *The Devil's Advocate* (dir. Guy Green), *Tess* (dir. Roman Polanski), *Madame Sousatzka* (dir. John Schlesinger), *Being Julia* (dir. István Szabó), and *Casanova* (dir. Lasse Hallström). His many television appearances include the lead roles in the series *Travelling Man* (Granada), *Kinsey* (BBC), and *Stick with Me, Kid* (Disney); plus numerous television shows, films, and mini-series in both England and America. He has directed plays in the UK and the USA.

His first book, *The Dream: An Actor's Story*, was published in 2008.

Leigh lives in London with his wife, actress and model, Twiggy. They have two children.

Now and Then is Leigh's first collection of poetry.

CW01496764

LEIGH LAWSON
NOW AND THEN

Flapjack Press
flapjackpress.co.uk
Exploring the synergy between performance and the page

Published in 2025 by Flapjack Press
Salford, Gtr Manchester
⊕ flapjackpress.co.uk · ▶ flapjackpress2520
f Flapjack Press · 𝕏 FlapjackPress

ISBN 978-1-0686052-3-9

Front cover photograph by Aron Visuals
⊕ unsplash.com/@aronvisuals

Back cover photograph by Brian Aris
⊕ brianaris.com

Design by Flapjack Press

Printed by Imprint Digital
Exeter, Devon
⊕ imprintdigital.com

A UNESCO City
of Literature

*The poems herein are dedicated to
Twiggs, Ace, Carly, and Saul,
my wonderful family and loved ones.
And to those I have loved who are
no longer at my table.*

*With special thanks to
Gyles Brandreth, Allie Esiri, Kitty Aldridge,
Caroline Hutton, and Paul Neads.*

Contents

Introduction

Dear Reader, I hope I may assume, as you have been kind enough to open this book and start reading, that we share a love of, or at least an interest in, poetry. I am not exactly sure when, or how, my passion for poetry was first seeded, but by my late teens poetry was firmly rooted in my psyche. My respect for, and love of, poetry deepened and broadened during my time as a drama student, firstly on a foundation course at Mountview Academy, and then continued as a full-time student at the Royal Academy of Dramatic Art in London, as I discovered the awesome power of the written and spoken word, particularly through verse.

Written over a period of many years, the earlier poems here are mostly assembled from old journals, the back pages of film, theatre and TV scripts, notebooks, etc. These early impressions and reflections in verse had, over a further period of time, migrated to a dark corner somewhere in my home, where they had been timidly hiding away too shy to show themselves. Two or three years ago, due to a house move, they emerged from their hiding place, and now join some more recent verses and musings in this little book.

Poetry has played an important part in my life, and I have often turned to poetry to make sense of my world, as both a reader and a writer. And yet, despite coming across various attempts to explain what poetry actually is, why it exists, and what compels someone to write a poem, I have never found a truly satisfying explanation to these questions. Neither, I'm afraid, am I able to offer you one. Interestingly though, it seems that most cultures since time immemorial have developed some form of poetry to elevate language to a level that cannot be reached by normal language alone, in the way that music sometimes can; poetry and music sharing the same DNA, that allows one to inspire the other so sublimely. I think it's fair to say that my eclectic taste in poetry has been almost as influenced by some of the great songwriters and lyricists, as much as by the poets I have grown to love.

To many people's surprise, Bob Dylan was awarded the Nobel Prize for Literature in 2016 for *"having created new poetic expressions within the Great American song tradition"*. This is a good example of how forms of poetry are changing, evolving, and broadening, but there are many more that have been ignored so far, and even frowned upon by the more snobbish elements of the academic literati in the poetry establishment. The poet, composer, and the songwriter are often concerned and united by the same issues and themes. Love, of course, birth and death, life itself, but also the wonders of nature, and the mysterious universe we all find ourselves a part of. Sometimes only poetry can get us anywhere near to understanding and expressing these emotions. Ben Johnson said *"poetry speaketh somewhat above a mortal mouth"*.

I make no personal claims of poetic accomplishment, merely a love and fascination with the written word in poetic form as a powerful and mysterious phenomenon. But I do fervently believe reading and writing poetry can have a positive effect on a person's wellbeing, and is good for heart, mind, and soul. Not least being the precious discovery: I am not alone. I am not the only one who feels like this! And maybe putting pen to paper is not for you at all. Maybe reading or listening is the correct prescription to sooth your ills, or face your demons, or celebrate your life.

As one grows older, golden memories become more treasured, and although not all memories are golden, most are remembered for a reason.

I suppose, in a way, some of the poems in this book could be viewed as memories; not always only the content of the poem, but also the time in my life when they insisted on being written, some real, some imagined. So I have taken the liberty to mirror and hopefully embellish some of the poems with a memory or comment or two, from around the time in my life when the poem appeared. Whilst not necessarily in chronological order, the contents chart some of the many journeys, observations, and reflections, as an actor, director, and writer, that began around the time I graduated from drama school in 1969, and continue to the present day. Hence the title of this small offering, which I sincerely hope you will enjoy picking up and reading – now and then.

"The ultimate aim of the poet should be to touch our hearts by showing his own."

—Thomas Hardy

Now and Then

Shortly after graduating from RADA, I was invited to Pinewood Studios to do a film test for the forthcoming film *Brother Sun, Sister Moon*, the story of Saint Francis of Assisi. The film to be directed by the famous, and somewhat infamous, Italian maestro Franco Zeffirelli, and shot entirely in Italy and Sicily. After the film test, I was offered the part of Saint Bernardo, one of the lead roles. My agent was told that shooting would not begin for at least six months. This turned out to be a very long and torturous journey that is addressed in much more detail in my first book, *The Dream: An Actor's Story*. But it did mean that I had a six-month period to fill, which also meant I could accept an offer of a couple of seasons, playing a variety of different roles, in three-weekly repertory at the Belgrade Theatre in Coventry. The Belgrade Theatre had an excellent reputation, and agreed to release me at a month's notice if the filming was brought forward for any reason. I had lived in Coventry for some time when I was growing up, before moving to London in my late teens.

Although my wages were barely enough to live on, I had a very happy and rewarding time at The Belgrade Theatre for two seasons, and two reasons. I was constantly meeting and working with new, talented actors and actresses to admire, and learn from, and also play some wonderful and diverse parts before returning to London, and eventually leaving for Italy to start filming *Brother Sun, Sister Moon,* which would occupy me for the next twelve months of my life. The poem 'Moses Backhouse' was my very first poem, it was written at the time when I returned to Coventry. Initially I was attracted simply by the name on the gravestone. No Wi-Fi or internet in 1969 of course, but on a whim I recently punched in the name "Moses Backhouse" on Google, and to my astonishment a picture of the very grave my poem refers to appeared, with some information about Moses Backhouse that I didn't know then at the time of writing ...

Moses Backhouse

An empty day in Coventry, aimlessly
Sauntering through the churchyard of Holy Trinity,
I chance upon a simple stone on the ground, lying prone;
The inscription tells me this is Moses Backhouse's final home.
It's as if this stone speaks to me
And was left there just for me to see.

Further down the hillside graduation
Veteran headstones stand at soldierly attention.
An old man rakes up the autumnal leaves,
The fallen dead from surrounding trees,
And adds them to a smoky fire
Like the grim reaper stoking his hellish pyre.

And they're raking the leaves
Off the grass that seeds
In the earth that feeds
On you Moses Backhouse.

My gaze is drawn back to the tablet on the grassy ground,
Dead leaves like pieces of old parchment lying all around.
Moses Backhouse 1843. Can this stone be speaking to me
Or is it his ghost with something to say,
Pointing now to an old stone tomb a few lives away?
I cross the narrow path to read the moss-dappled epitaph.

Did you see this inscription Moses when you passed this way,
Just a few steps from where you now lay?

Alfred Hammerton	*9 weeks*	*1833*
Edward Hammerton	*11 years*	*1834*
Maria Hammerton	*20 years*	*1840*
Elizabeth Hammerton	*19 years*	*1841*

Did you know young Elizabeth or Maria perhaps?
Did you hold her warm hand and walk down Hilltop?
Did you kiss her lips on a day like today
Before they were cold and turned to decay?
That maiden you may have brought posies
Would not thrill you now old Moses.

"Now get you to my lady's chamber
And tell her, let her paint an inch thick,
To this favour she must come"
Thus said the bard right and just,
"Golden lads and girls all must,
As chimney sweepers, come to dust."

And they're scraping the leaves
Off the grass that seeds
In the earth that feeds
On you Moses Backhouse.

My childish fears fall to the ground in selfish tears
And join the scrum of ghostly leaves
As if I somehow had been bereaved.
I stand and weep among the too-young dead
Grateful I still have my whole life ahead
To strut and fret my hour upon the stage

And then be heard no more.
And I notice at my feet of clay
The leaves are dancing the dance of death today
And for a sacred moment there is no earthly sound
Whilst whispered thoughts become unreasonably profound
On this patch of hallowed ground

In the Hilltop churchyard with no church
In the Warwickshire town,
Ancient headstones all around.
Who were you? I wonder, now resting this long-time sleep,
Sharing with mouldy bedfellows a worn, green blanket
And patched leafy counterpane?

   And they're scraping the leaves
   Off the grass that seeds
   In the earth that feeds
   On you Moses Backhouse.

Lives fade and perish like an autumn leaf
Falling silent onto a grave beneath,
Whilst worms devour what life endows.
God rest you still, and give you peace,
Old Moses Backhouse.

When arriving in Italy in 1970 to play the role of Bernardo in *Brother Sun, Sister Moon*, I was welcomed by a group of fellow young actors who had already started filming, some of whom have remained friends to this day. The film took over a year to shoot in various parts of Italy and Sicily, and we group of young actors formed a strong bond together, and subsequently spent a lot of our spare time in each other's company playing our guitars and making up songs. The summer months were scorching hot, and the winter months were bitterly cold; our heads were tonsured and we were required, whilst filming, to wear thin sackcloth cassocks and nothing on our feet. The days were long and hard, scrabbling around barefoot over snow-covered rocks and stones from dawn to dusk. Trying to appear on camera as if we didn't mind the cold, discomfort, and pain in the slightest was a major acting discipline that they had failed to prepare us for at drama school.

I travelled with my guitar in those days and for some years afterwards. This poem is structured on the page as a calligram to suggest the neck and fretboard of a guitar ...

On Playing Guitar with a Friend

A
Friend
A consolation
Worth a year of
Hours
A life of
Ours.
A tune of life
Of hours
Of ours.
Strum, stringing through
Sounds
Umbiliconcordance
Always
A
Sweet sound,
Accord.
A
Chord
Strumming through
Mellowed
Never changing, changing ever
Picking
Fretting
Keyed up.
Notifying
Each other.

There is a wonderful poem called 'Naming of Parts' by Henry Reed. The poem is about a young National Service solider in a military classroom being instructed on the names and component parts that make up a rifle, but he is finding it hard to concentrate and keeps getting distracted by the view from the window.

Luckily for me (and the Army), National Service was abolished in the UK about a year or so before I would have been due for call up. Although I was never in the military, my schooldays, and time spent in a classroom, were not the happiest days of my life, and quite a lot of my time was spent gazing out of classroom windows, daydreaming. This preoccupation with daydreaming began very early on in my life, and I continued to find the school classes a great inconvenience and interruption to my preferred occupation of gazing out of the window and at least letting my imagination run riot.

When I was about twelve or thirteen years old, at school assembly (held every morning for school announcements, prayers, and hymns), my friend Ronald Shufflebottom and I would constantly be in trouble with the patrolling teachers for making up our own versions of the words, and sometimes tunes, to the hymns being sung. We found this hilarious. The teachers did not. So we would inevitably end up in detention after school, being forced to write out endless pages of the correct words to the hymns; many of which I have since grown to love, and I realise now were a wonderful introduction and precursor to my love of poetry. I am told that years later, when I became a bit well known as an actor, a red ribbon was tied around a leg of my school desk as a mark of achievement. How this came about remains a mystery, as I do not recall there being any prizes awarded at the time for daydreaming.

Poetry becoming an important part of my life has inevitably led to quite a large collection of poetry books. I have an eclectic taste in poetry, some more conventional from well-known poets, some more unconventional and less well known. All have had an influence on my life, and all hold a special place in my heart.

Some years after writing this poem, and quite by chance whilst researching the works of Frances Bacon, I came across this quote:

> *"Some books should be tasted, some devoured, but only*
> *a few should be chewed and digested thoroughly."*
> —Frances Bacon, *1561-1626*

Sunday Breakfast in Bed

I lie in my bed with books that I've read
Gathered around me, I'm so glad they found me,
Breakfast in bed with someone I've read,
Others unknown that I've invited home.

Poems for Life, an anthology,
Flashes its title and winks at me,
The World of Kabbalah attempts to explain all;
I found them last week on a market stall.

John Betjeman's *Summoned by Bells*,
Reflections in verse of his life he tells.
Dylan Thomas's poems, tales, and other glories,
I can hear his mellifluous voice telling me stories.

Larkin, Frost, Cummings also appear,
McNiece, the Brownings, Duffy, Lear.
Great voices all around, virtuosity in sound,
The bitter, the sweet, the trivial and profound.

A feast of words. A banquet on a blanket.
The mouth-watering aroma as a page is turned over,
The delicate taste of a well-turned phrase
Cries look at me, I'm beautiful, from every page.

Poems, verses, voices speak to me and enthral,
Henri, Patten, McGough, oh how I love you all,
Tasty delicious new morsels not yet read
Languishing there for the picking on my picnic bed.

Aromas blend, stun, stimulate, saturate, and even enrage,
Soak the senses, rise to the skies, and dive, page after page,
Too deep to fathom, too large to hold, too finite to touch,
A helter-skelter from hell to heaven, at times almost too much.

Outside of my window it's cold, dull, and uninviting,
But inside, my bed is a hotbed, seething and exciting,
An orgy of discovery sets my senses wildly reeling.
Am I awake or am I dreaming?

As noon approaches, I'm still feeding
On poems and verses, I can't stop reading.
Is it time to clear them all away, or
Shall I stay in bed and feast all day?

I lie in my bed with books that I've read
Gathered around me, I'm so glad they found me,
Breakfast in bed with someone I've read,
Others unknown that I've invited home.

After a year serving my apprenticeship in film-making, working on *Brother Sun, Sister Moon* in Italy with the maestro Zeffirelli, I returned to England. I was fortunate to find myself in the position of receiving a steady flow of scripts and offers of work, mostly in film and TV. But privately, I longed to return to my first love – the theatre. I guess the grass is always greener on the other side. Most of my young actor friends doing theatre were longing to be offered some film roles, and I was constantly envious of their life in the theatre. Although, one of the highlights at this time was when I was invited to join the cast of a TV film for ABC America, called *Love Among the Ruins*. It was to be directed by the legendary Hollywood director George Cukor, and to star Katherine Hepburn and Laurence Olivier in the leading roles. I was offered the wonderful part of Alfred Pratt, the juvenile lead, after meeting (and subsequent approval of) Miss Hepburn. It was all shot in England, and when it was released in America won several Emmys and other awards. For a young actor to work with such giants as Cukor, Olivier, and Hepburn so early on in his career, apart from being a bit overwhelming, was a lucky break, and once or twice afterwards I was very flattered, surprised, and grateful to be told that Olivier had generously recommended me for a role in various productions.

During filming I got to know, and got on especially well with, the great Katherine Hepburn – or Kate as she asked me to call her. We would talk often during the set-up times between shots about life, acting, theatre, poetry, and what appeared to be her favourite subject, the great actor and love of her life, Spencer Tracy, whom she lived with, loved, and adored for many years, but never married.

Around this time, another milestone and turning point in my life was when I made my first appearance in a West End theatre in a play called *A Touch of Spring*, at the Comedy Theatre, playing the marvellous scene-stealing role of Baldo. My leading lady on this occasion was the incredibly talented and beautiful actress Hayley Mills, who had been a star since she was twelve years old and was now in her late twenties. During the run, Hayley and I fell deeply in love and moved in to live together. Following the example of Hepburn and Tracy we also never married, but spent ten wonderful years together before deciding to go our separate ways. Almost fifty years later we remain friends and devoted grandparents to our three grandchildren. When you want to say how much you love someone, there are few ways that surpass poetry to express the language of love. This poem was read at our granddaughter's blessing in 2018, about a year after she was born. The Latin title means "Much in Little" …

Multum in Parvo

You're the pulse of every heartbeat,
The wings that let me fly,
You're the sad that makes me laugh,
The happy that makes me cry.

You're a sunburst, you're a moonbeam,
You're a starry starry night,
Another wonder of creation
That Mother Nature got just right.

You're a secret wish, a guilty pleasure,
A thing beyond compare.
You're that something in the street
That makes people stop and stare.

You're the opium of the masses,
You're as sacred as a Mass is,
You're psilocybin and you're hashish,
You're what happens when lightning flashes.

You're the twinkle in my eye,
The wish before I die,
You're the answer to all life's questions,
You're the When? The How? The Why?

My first visit to the magical country of India in 1974 was to join Marianne Faithfull, Dame Penelope Keith, and a cast of British actors for the film *Ghost Story*. My second visit to India was in 1987 to join Kirk Douglas, Sarah Miles, and Claire Bloom, amongst others, to shoot the American mini-series *Queenie* for ABC America. In between, in 1975, I had also been in the equally magical country of Sri Lanka, the tiny island off the southern tip of India once known as Ceylon. I was there for several months playing the title role in the film *The God King*. It is in India and Sri Lanka where I first experienced the power of meditation.

On one full moon, or Poya night, as it is known in Sri Lanka, an old man I had never met before appeared at my lodgings and informed me that he had been told, in a dream, to take me to meditate and pray at the Temple of "The Sacred Bodhi Tree", believed to be a descendant of the tree in India that the Buddha received enlightenment under. This experience changed my life. At the Temple, he taught me a simple prayer that I recite still to this day at full moon ...

Samsara

Something, unworldly, transcendental,
Had happened this time there,
The ancient sounds of mountains, rivers,
Drums and cicadas suffused the evening air.

When the chanting and meditation ceased
After the preparation of the feast,
The people gathered around the wise man,
The swami, the sage, the priest.

"Tell us of time," asked someone of the sage.
"Time does not exist, no start, no end, no age.
Why are you in the world at this time and not any other?
This is all you need to discover."

"What is love?" asked another.
"Love is the child of the soul," he replied,
"Love, time, life, are not of man's making.
They cannot be seen, but must not be forsaken."

"Then what is life if not of man's making?"
The wise man smiled and gently said,
"Your life is a gift, do not be mistaken.
It cannot be bought but it can be taken."

"What then of death?" asked an old man.
"Death and birth are the same, one as another,
Both the end and beginning.
Death is born like a child to a mother."

The people gathered there that day
Are confused by the words they hear,
But "Words," said the sage, "like thoughts or prayer,
Like birds of the air, fly away and disappear."

Later when the people returned from the feast
With more questions for the wise man, the swami, the priest,
He, like words, thoughts or prayer,
Like birds ascending into the air,
Had disappeared and was no longer there.

The poet Philip Larkin famously wrote *"They fuck you up, your mum and dad"* in his poem 'This Be the Verse'; I'm inclined to agree with him. My father was an alcoholic monster, but thank God I had an angel for a mother. She kept me on the straight and narrow when I could have so easily stepped over the line into juvenile delinquency as a youngster.

As sometimes happens with poetry, it helps to write things down. But even now I still find this poem painful and hard to read ...

David and Goliath

How well do I remember,
The memories haunt me still,
And though I hoped that they would fade
I know now they never will.

The myriad occasions that should have
But were not filled with joy,
Destroyed by a demonic father
When I was a boy.

I cannot forget one dark day
When I was still a lad,
Fuelled with rage, or fear, or both,
Throwing out my dad.

He'd been bullying my mother,
Hit her, made her cry.
I threw him to the ground and said,
"I wish you'd crawl away and die."

He lay there in the porch way.
Why didn't he retaliate at all?
I was just a pubescent kid,
He, over six feet tall.

I know not to this day why he chose
To not fight back,
And smash me to the ground
After my attack.

"You can't do that to me," he said,
"I'm your father," was his only sound,
But there was a new understanding
Betwixt us. As he lay there on the ground.

Curtains twitched at neighbours' windows
As he rose to his full height,
My knees were knocking, but my fists were clenched
To continue with the fight.

But instead he turned and walked away
Without a backward glance.
I trembled and shook from head to foot
That I'd taken such a chance.

But I felt no pleasure,
No sense of victory, in heart or head.
I felt disgraced, I felt ashamed,
And wished that I was dead.

I still feel shame to this day
For the things I did and said,
But a mother is a mother and a son is a son,
And he has a duty to protect her when all is said and done.

In 1977 I was offered the role of Giacomo Nerone in the feature film *The Devil's Advocate*. The film was based on the novel by Morris West, directed by Guy Green, and starring John Mills, Stephane Audran, and Pulitzer Prize- and Tony Award-winning actor and writer Jason Miller, who became a great friend and something of a mentor. A true man of the theatre; clever, gifted, and tortured. Whilst I was filming *The Devil's Advocate* in Germany, Hayley gave birth to our son in London. Thanks to a clause in my contract, I was allowed to fly home to the UK for two days to meet my son. He was named Jason after my new friend, but he has always been known to one and all by his family name of "Ace" – because that's what he is.

I was thrilled to be a father but I was more than a little apprehensive, because I had no template, no role model, of how to be a good dad. However, despite this, something seems to have gone right as I have been blessed with a son and friend who has become a brilliant father himself, and whom I love beyond words.

In 1982 I shot my second movie in Germany called *Fire and Sword*, the story of Tristan and Isolde, starring Christoph Waltz and Antonia Preser as the fateful lovers. My role was that of King Mark and I was very pleased to also have my dear old friend and godfather to my son, the fine actor Peter Firth, working on this film with me, our second of three films together. I'm told that *Fire and Sword* won a cinematography award at Catalonia's Sitges Film Festival, but I have to confess to actually never watching either of these films. Watching myself on screen is not something I enjoy and avoid whenever possible.

As a footnote to the above and lead-in to this next poem, an interview I did in the UK whilst I was promoting *Fire and Sword* appeared with my photograph in a newspaper that was seen by my father. I had not been in touch with him for over twenty-five years since my parents separated, but he contacted me, asking if we could meet. It was a very emotional reunion. We made our peace, and somehow I found I could forgive the sad old man I met for ruining my childhood. Forgive but not forget ...

You Gave Me None of That

How to kick a football,
Hold a cricket bat,
How to swim or ride a bicycle,
You gave me none of that.

How to do a magic trick,
Lay a toy railway track
Or a visit to a theatre,
You gave me none of that.

I have no memory of holidays shared
Or a father and son chat,
No dinner or lunch at restaurants,
You gave me none of that.

I could go on, the list is long
Of what you failed at,
But love was what I missed the most,
You gave me none of that.

You once gave me a pair of boxing gloves
And taught me how to scrap,
It came in useful once or twice,
So thanks at least for that.

There is very little else for which
My thanks are due, in fact.
What I needed was a hand to hold,
Some guidance or road map
On how to be a father,
But you gave me none of that.

Over the years I have crossed paths with quite a few people who, at some point, dreamed of a life in the arts before deciding on a safer, more secure, profession. Many seem to have retained a longing or regret for the road not taken. I personally have never for a moment regretted taking the road less travelled, although there have been times when nothing can prepare you for the way the dice will fall. My first book, *The Dream: An Actor's Story*, finishes at around the time I was planning to direct a new version I had written of a theatre piece called *Noël and Gertie*, the story of Noël Coward and Gertrud Lawrence. My version was retitled *If Love Were All*, and starred my gorgeous and multitalented wife Twiggy, whom I had married in 1988. The show premiered in 1998 at The Bay Street Theatre in Sag Harbour, Long Island, New York, to great reviews and, just as thrillingly, the promise of a transfer to an Off-Broadway theatre.

After the successful run at Bay Street we flew home to the UK to await confirmation as to when the theatre would become available for us to transfer our show to New York City. Our bags were packed and there had been an announcement in the press that we were transferring. Then I received a phone call one morning to tell me that the $1million promised to fund the transfer had fallen through. We were gutted. Devastated. What to do? I quickly realised we had two choices. Choice one – accept the situation, open a bottle of wine, and get drunk and depressed. Or choice two – try and raise the money ourselves and get the show on. We chose the latter. I made some phone calls to people I thought might be interested in investing, and by the end of the day we had raised $350,000. Within ten days we had the full amount.

The show opened at the Lucille Lortel Theatre with Twiggy, who had previously had a huge success and Tony nomination on Broadway in the musical *My One and Only*, and Harry Groaner, who was a greatly respected Broadway performer and two-times Tony award winner. The man who joined us as executive producer, Julian Schlossberg, brought onboard some more investors and expertly steered us through the minefield of putting on a play, and furthermore made the whole experience a pleasure and a joy, and became a very dear lifelong friend.

At the first preview in New York the audience rose to their feet at the curtain call, cheering and shouting for more. *The New York Times* review was a love letter to Twiggy's magic on stage, and the critics proclaimed the two performers *"charming, sexy, dazzling, sublime, beguiling, delightful, divine"* – their words, not mine. We were a hit. All the investors got a return on their investment and a profit was made. It was my baptism of fire in becoming a producer. There's no Business like this Business known as Show! True to say, getting the show on was a long and, at times, torturous journey. But finally to have the show running in New York that I had written, directed, and co-produced was an overwhelmingly gratifying feeling and well worth the pain.

When this poem first appeared I was thinking about someone who was a gifted guitar player and painter. As a young man he had chosen his profession in law for safety and security, and to please his parents, who referred to a creative life in the arts as "not a proper job". He had lamented his entire working life that he hadn't pursued his dream ...

The Song Unsung

He wanted to paint pictures
    Like Picasso or Lucian Freud,
Create something of beauty
    But that still got folk annoyed.

He wanted to write songs
    Like McCartney and Wings,
Verses that tell a story
    And make people want to sing.

He hoped he hadn't left it too late
    To pick up a palette, a brush and paint.
He hoped he still had time
    To jot down some verses that rhyme.

But he waited just a bit too long
    Before he wrote his famous song,
And he didn't invest in canvas, paint or brush
    Because other things were in such a rush.

So when his time was finally up
    And the grandfather clock had terminally struck,
There was still a gap on the wall at the RA and Tate
    Because he'd left it all too late,

And the music that he so longed
    To compose for his famous song
Was replaced by a well-known hymn that was played
    As they bore his coffin along.

Best not postpone 'til tomorrow
    What could be done today,
'Cos time and tide wait for no man
    Or so the proverbs say.

In 1990, after a successful run in London playing Antonio opposite Dustin Hoffman as Shylock in Shakespeare's *The Merchant of Venice*, directed by Sir Peter Hall, the show transferred to New York and gave me my first taste of Broadway as an actor.

Before going to New York, and during the London run of the play, the world's greatest English-speaking actor, Laurence Olivier, who had been so supportive to me as a young actor, sadly died. That night all London West End theatres dimmed their lights as a mark of respect and affection for the great man. It was decided that a two-minute silence would be held at the curtain call of all West End shows that night. Although we were playing to sell-out, very appreciative, audiences at every performance in London, in Britain audiences at that time very rarely got to their feet for a standing ovation at a straight play curtain call. Opera yes, ballet yes, but rarely drama, unlike Broadway, who are much more likely to give a standing ovation to a successful play.

On the day of Olivier's death, I was, as usual, standing next to Dustin as we took our curtain call and he announced the two minutes of silence to the audience. We then stood in line for what seemed like the longest imaginable two-minute silence. The atmosphere was electric and, fanciful as it sounds, one could almost feel the presence of Olivier in the auditorium. He had made his West End debut in this very theatre, The Phoenix, with Noël Coward in the premiere of his play *Private Lives* in 1939. My mother was manageress of this theatre at that time. When the two-minute silence was over, the whole audience simultaneously rose to their feet and burst into spontaneous applause for the great actor. As we turned to exit the stage into the wings, Dustin looked at me over his shoulder and, with a twinkle in his eye, whispered to me, *"Is that what you have to do to get a standing ovation in this country – fucking die?"* We all loved Dustin, his humour, generosity, and love of his craft helped us through many a crisis.

In New York we got a standing ovation at every performance.

I love America, and particularly I love New York. New York has been good to me. I love playing Broadway. Broadway has been kind to me. For the Broadway run I had to find an apartment to stay in. I rented a place on the Upper West Side, near to an old actress friend. She was once a Broadway star, and sacrificed everything for her career. No husband, no children. She hadn't been offered any stage work for a long time. She told me one day, *"I think the parade has passed me by."* Showbusiness can be a cruel business ...

Silver Frames

A life passes through
    The streets of Manhattan,
A west side story, shadows,
    And memories all but forgotten.

Photograph frames crowd an apartment shelf
    Where she sits by herself
In a room where friends used to blend,
    With music and white sofas, but that's at an end.

No baby toys, no children noise,
    Sepia-filled silver frames and spaces
Of what could have, should have been.
    A barren land, seedless things. No hers, no hims.

I returned to London from New York in 2002 after appearing on Broadway in the brilliant farce *Noises Off* by Michael Frayn. I was asked by the director, Jeremy Sams, to play the same role in a production for the Royal National Theatre in the West End in London. I was at home polishing up on the script when I heard a song on the radio coming from the next room. I stopped working on the script and this poem appeared instead.

A dear friend who is one of the world's all-time greatest performers, songwriters, and lyricists, and who was kind enough to read some of my verses, suggested a change, so I have incorporated his suggestion. After all, who am I to disagree with the genius talent of the man who wrote 'Yesterday' ...

I Would Have Called

I would have called but I have fears
    I remind you of unhappy years.
I heard our song again today,
    Played on the radio by an old DJ.

My God, how potent that song was
    When we were young and lost in love,
When all of life was spread before us,
    And we knew every word, verse and chorus.

Did only the music survive when our love died?
    I would have called but I have fears,
I remind you of unhappy years.
    An album cover stained with tears.

In 1994 I played the part of Deely in Harold Pinter's three-hander play *Old Times*, opposite Julie Christie and Dame Harriet Walter, directed by the brilliant Australian teacher and director, Lindy Davies. This was one of those very enjoyable and fulfilling experiences that sometimes come along and make you very glad that you became an actor. The production opened in a small theatre in Clwyd in North Wales. Clwyd is surrounded by ancient rocky landscapes. We transferred to the less ancient, and less rocky, landscape of London's West End for a very successful sell-out run. We were then invited to Russia to do the play at an arts festival in Moscow, where the play was again rapturously received. Wales to London, and then to Moscow, was an unusual and remarkable theatrical journey.

Wales has a long association with a love of the spoken word, albeit the Welsh spoken word. Every year an Eisteddfod is held when people compete in a poetry festival. Dylan Thomas is one of Wales's most famous poets. He chose to write in English, and in the early 1960s I fell totally, and entirely, under the spell of this wordsmith extraordinaire.

In the summer of 2018, I went on a pilgrimage to the very beautiful village of Laugharne (pronounced "Larn") where Thomas lived and wrote a lot of his later work. Laugharne is a tiny but magical place with a ruined castle overlooking the bay. I stayed in Brown's Hotel, where Thomas used to go every day to get drunk, and if given the chance, recite his poetry in the bar. I visited the small hut overlooking the bay where he wrote his most famous play, *Under Milk Wood*, inspired by Laugharne itself. I walked the walks referenced in his poems, and visited his simple hillside grave. Reading Dylan Thomas in Laugharne brought me closer to my hero, in much the same way that speaking Shakespeare's lines on the stage of the Royal Shakespeare Company Theatre in Stratford-upon-Avon feels like the proper and perfect place to be doing so ...

The Ghost of Laugharne
(Ode to Dylan Thomas)

In Laugharne, lounging in the bar of Brown's Hotel,
For the price of a whisky or beer
He would poems recite and stories tell.
In a worn three-piece suit of shabby tweed,
Hair curly as cockles, wild as the seas,
His mellifluous voice could make your heart bleed.

A cigarette hung from his voluble lips,
Removed to talk or take generous sips.
But talent oozed from every alcoholic pore
And when he ceased the crowd would call for more.
His stamina, and consumption, knew no bounds,
As long as others in the bar were buying the rounds.

A young life endured in a poet's penury,
Wearing second-hand cast-offs clothed and shod,
A tortured genius, with a gift from God.
That gift could transform the spoken word into song
But destiny decreed it would not be for long,
The desire for oblivion in him too strong.

And in that bar, at Brown's Hotel,
The one-man Eisteddfod was a bottomless well,
But with oblivion, the Welsh poet's only true friend,
And with more free drinks from fair-weather friends,
He would fall in a drunken stupor to the ground,
To laughter and applause from those gathered around.

Until that dubious lady fate caused his tormented spirit to rise,
His poems found favour before influential eyes.
Courted by America to give some recitals,
By a group of admirers with posh names and titles.
His readings proved to be a resounding success,
Fame in the media, reviewed in the press.

But then one liquor-soaked day in that land far away,
He consumed a lethal amount of whisky, they say.
And at the Chelsea Hotel in New York city,
His best friend Oblivion showed him no pity.
And the golden boyo with a heavenly voice and vocabulary
Breathed his last and ceased to be.

Too soon the troubled troubadour is gone,
But still his stories and his verse live on
In the ruined castle town known as Laugharne,
Suffused, as it yet still is, with the Welsh Bard's charm.
Rains splutter words from drainpipes into gutters
His face stares dumbly from behind the hotel shutters.

Cottages stand like stanzas in a row,
The bay water laps in iambic rhapsody to and fro,
Seabirds screech his name over land and seas,
Lost words drift from treetops like autumnal leaves
Seeking a home, searching for their time,
Hungry for a mouth to shape them into rhyme,

Looking for the ghost of Laugharne.
Today, on a steep sleepy slope above the town,
A white wooden cross that bears his name is gazing down.
Oblivion, finally, on this familiar beloved hillside,
Overlooking the town that bleeds
And breathes his name with pride.
Trees, hedgerows, and bushes bristle,
Horses bray and songbirds whistle,

Their melodies full-blown, carefree, in everlasting remembering
Of the small hunched town, and the ghost of Laugharne's story
To weep, wallow, mourn and rejoice in the dead poet's glory.
Flying his name over Milk Wood and Fern Hill
Bearing the birthday dreams of the Welsh bard,
To oceans and skies – and set fire to the stars.

Wales has a unique landscape, majestic and serene, rugged and mountainous, wild streams and beautiful beaches. There are also a great many medieval castles in Wales, several of which were used as locations whilst filming the movie *Sword of the Valiant*. I remember many days in armour, endless sword fights, and hours gallivanting around on a very large horse in the rain. A much gentler experience was rehearsing Pinter's play *Old Times* in Clwyd, North Wales. This was an altogether extremely happy experience, and walking on air to the theatre, or back to my lodgings after the show, through this ancient land is a memory I will always treasure ...

A Walk in Wales

Well might thou in troubled flight
Flee the long dank bright
Dappling dungeon of unknown tributes
Lost in languages not now spoken.
Flee then flee all and thee,
But leaving mountain wood and tree,
Departing struggle, wriggle like worms
In fishermen's pot
Or maggots to flies disguise the plot.
Beaver dams disrupted trickles,
Budding branches troubled weeds,
Clogged, blocked from needs to seeds,
Algorithms writing wrongs, woofing warbles
Nature's song.
Clamber up, struggle down,
Over dust, rocks, stones in rubble-bubble
Sink to fish stare. Stopping clocks.
Ah, but time dictating plot.
Fiddles, dribbles, cares not.
Gives not, takes all,
Delving, seeking, turning, call.
Searching, finding, hearing, all.

The story of Gawain and the Green Knight was made into the film *Sword of the Valiant*, directed by Stephen Weeks, whom I had worked with on the movie *Ghost Story* in India some years earlier. For this film Stephen cast me in the part of Humphrey, squire to Sir Gawain, played by Miles O'Keeffe. Sean Connery starred as the Green Knight and a host of other well-known and respected actors including Trevor Howard, Peter Cushing, Lila Kedrova, and the beautiful French actress, Cyrielle Clair.

When I was a young boy our heroes in the movies were cowboys on horseback or knights in shining armour. During the shooting of *Sword of the Valiant* in Wales, Ireland, and France, I was thrilled to be made an honorary stuntman for my sword-fighting and horse-riding skills, and given an impressive badge to prove it ...

The Knight's Creed

I am a good friend. A dangerous foe.
I will help beyond the bounds of generosity
But mar and wound with unusual ferocity,
With all the power that God hath given me.

Do harm to me or mine
There will be vengeance to the point of crime.
Show me love and kindness,
My return of same is boundless.

Some deeds are to forgive but not forget,
Yet there is justice in reproof;
An eye for an eye,
A tooth for a tooth.

I choose to not forget.
To remember is a warning.
A shield. Armour. A sword.
I use them in attack. I use them in defending.

I forgive because I must,
Hate has never furnished
A satisfying counsel. Strong or weak,
I do not turn the other cheek.

I choose not to live with contempt
But stay my creed and not relent.
To seek, to find, a peace sublime.
To err is human, to forgive divine.

I have spent a great deal of my adult life living in hotels in various parts of the world whilst shooting a movie, TV series, or touring with a show. Although travelling can be interesting and fun, being separated from loved ones can be very tough at times. When I now look back at some of the poems I have written over the time I have been an actor, I can see that a great many were written when I was away from home, on location somewhere in the world, sometimes for very long periods. These are my lonely poems. Taking into account that the majority of the twenty-or-so feature films I have appeared in were mostly shot away from my home in the UK, plus theatre tours, British and American TV films, series and shows, a world tour with the Royal Shakespeare Company, and several productions on Broadway, plus many American mini-series, it has meant a great deal of time living out of a suitcase. In between, there were many other shorter periods on the road away from my home in London, and that's not to say many were very enjoyable times too. I have mostly loved being an actor, director, and writer, and have been very fortunate to work pretty consistently, and see the world whilst practising my craft. But it can at times be a strain on all sorts of relationships. I have found reading and writing poetry to be a great consolation and comfort during these times ...

Without You

Without you
   I lie in the sun and stay white,
Without you
   The days are shorter than the night
And the days are long
   Without you.

Without you
   A bath is just having a wash,
Without you
   A beach buggy is noisy and uncomfortable
And it's boring
   Without you

Without you
   Wherever I am, I don't want to be,
Don't want to
   Swim, play tennis, sail, run,
Watch a film or TV
   Without you.

Without you
   I drink too much,
Smoke too much,
   Eat too much,
Spend too much
   Time on my own
Without you.

When I first started writing poetry, I was in repertory theatre. I was playing a different role every three weeks, rehearsing one role during the day whilst playing another in the evening and matinées. I was being paid ten pounds ten shillings a week. If it was cold and I didn't have a shilling left for the gas fire in my lodging room, I went to bed fully clothed with my script to keep warm whilst learning my lines. I was so happy to be working as a professional actor and playing some wonderful parts that I didn't mind the poverty of no heat and little food.

I realise now how fortunate I was to just catch the end of a period when most major cities and towns in the UK had their own permanent theatre repertory companies. In those early days in rep, the experience of playing such a wide variety of roles was fantastically valuable as an actor. A new and completely different character, genre, style, and period every three weeks from Shakespeare, Restoration, Farce, to Chekhov, Shaw, Becket, and Pinter, to Agatha Christie, and Pantomime; an invaluable apprenticeship.

I promised myself I would endeavour, for the rest of my acting or directing career, to return to the theatre whenever practical and possible.

I will always remember with great affection and gratitude those days in rep, in various cities around the country, and have never felt a greater conviction that I had chosen well, or been chosen, to live the life I was living than when I was in a theatre, or on tour in a play. Of course, there were also some sad times, and when I look now at these next few poems I am reminded of the heartache that goes hand in glove with being away from home and family. Life and love hold many surprises, some pleasant, some not. Some good, some not so good. But always, always for an actor, whatever the experience, a realisation that one day you will probably be called upon to draw on, and more than likely use, all of these emotions in attempting to channel, portray, and express what you are trying to convey to an audience, whether tragic, or comic; these emotions so clearly depicted by our professional emblem, the two masks of Melpomene and Thalia, the symbols of tragedy and comedy from as far back as Greek theatre.

Sometimes, when rehearsing or playing a role, a poem appears as a result of an emotion or experience triggered by the character you are portraying. Real or imagined – sometimes love hurts ...

Yesterdays

Then you came. Washing over today
Like yesterday never happened.
Making tomorrow always today,
And today everything.
Tomorrow need never come,
But sometimes it did.
Sometimes it did.

No night or day, only light or dark,
Or change of time, for those
Who were not us to sleep,
I remember the sun time was longer
In passing than the moon time,
But not much.
Not much.

Then you found your way out of
Our tangle of troubled trespass
On a yesterday daytime,
Just as the sun was waking from sleep,
Too late to call back yesterday.
Too late.
Too late.

In 1988 I was pleased to join the cast of Shirley MacLaine, Peggy Ashcroft, Twiggy, and Shabana Azmi, to play the role of Ronnie Blum in the film *Madame Sousatzka*, directed by John Schlesinger. John was a lovely man whom I had admired as a director for a long time, and became a good friend. He lived quite close to us in London, and I remember many wonderful dinner parties at his house, always with glamorous guests, fabulous food and wine, and lots and lots of laughter.

Lunch or dinner around a table with a group of friends, be it at home or on location, is one of my favourite ways of spending time. Many of my musician and theatre friends love telling and hearing stories and jokes on such occasions, which suits me fine, as laughing together is surely one of life's great pleasures. I remember John loving the following story when I told it to him:

> An elderly couple had dinner at another couple's house, and after eating, the wives left the table and went into the kitchen.
>
> The two gentlemen were talking, and one said, "Last night we went out to a new restaurant and it was really great. I would recommend it very highly."
>
> The other man said, "What is the name of the restaurant?"
>
> The first man thought and thought and finally said, "What is the name of that flower you give to someone you love? You know. The one that's red and has thorns."
>
> "Do you mean a rose?"
>
> "Yes, that's the one," replied the man. He then turned towards the kitchen and yelled to his wife, "Rose, what's the name of that restaurant we went to last night?"

Sometimes life and love can all get a bit sombre and serious, and poetry, like life, should not be devoid of humour. Although this joke did not inspire my poem, there is a tenuous connection via the equally prickly subjects of love and roses ...

Rusty Roses

The roses you sent me died today,
    I tried to revive them in the kitchen sink
But those white roses refused to drink.
    They died, dried, no fragrance, no colour,
Turned into faded chrysalids of each other.

I would have preferred red roses or even pink,
    Perhaps they wouldn't have died in the kitchen sink.
Oh why did you send roses of white?
    White roses turn to rust,
They mark an end, not beginning, for us.

The roses you sent me died today,
    So did our love by the way;
It died, dried, no fragrance, no colour.
    Face it, we got things so wrong.
From bud, to rose, to rust, did not take long.

Gossip columns in newspapers and magazines thrive on reports of actors falling in and out of love with their leading man or woman – or both. Sometimes love survives after the play or film, sometimes not. Mostly not ...

Gone

Love don't live here anymore.
Packed its bags. Walked out the door.
Wanted something. Not this for sure.
Love don't live here anymore.

Who knows how? Who knows why?
Something killed it. Cruel goodbye.
What was there does not remain.
His fault? Hers? None can claim.

There's a note pinned to the door.
                    It says
Love don't live here anymore.

After a successful run in London's West End in the play *Art* by Yasmina Reza, we took it on a tour of the UK. I loved this play. I loved it so much that I did two runs in the West End, both times followed by a UK tour. *Art* threw up a great many subjects for examination – like friendship, background, education, and of course art itself. It can be a lonely life on the road, but a great opportunity to read and write. I always keep an anthology of poetry by my bedside at home, I also travel with one when going away. I find it a great companion.

One day whilst on tour I came across a poem by Thomas Hood called 'I Remember, I Remember'. I first read this poem when I was a boy at school. It appears to be a disillusioned, unhappy adult, longing for the return of his happy childhood. For me, the reverse is true. After a miserable childhood, I have sought, and mostly found, happiness as an adult. In reading the poem as a boy, and then later, I was of course struck by its melancholy, but remember also being envious of the comfortable sounding security of the poet's life as a middle-class, small boy, in a lovely house, and how that childhood contrasted so starkly with my own working-class background. So I wrote this poem as both a deliberate contrast, tribute, and pastiche of Thomas Hood's poem, but reflecting my own childhood.

Philip Larkin also wrote a poem entitled 'I Remember', ironically about Coventry, which is the "big city" referred to in this poem ...

I Remember I Remember

I remember I remember
The house where I was born,
Freezing cold in winter,
No heat to keep us warm.
Cockroaches thrived in our kitchen,
The only loo was out in the backyard,
Our tin bath hung on the wall outside,
Life was very hard.

I remember I remember
We played where bombs had dropped,
Decimating everything,
Houses, factories, shops,
Then we played among the ruins,
In the ruins of what we'd lost.
Now there's an irony worth considering
When you come to count the cost.

I remember I remember
A violent father, drunk most every night,
Abusing my saintly mother,
Ending in a fight.
Planning how to stop him,
Stab him with a knife?
Spend my life in prison?
I would have gladly paid the price.

I remember I remember
The bully 'round our way,
He'd wait for me at the top of the street
When I went out to play.
I grabbed him by his hair one day
And punched him in the face.
He didn't wait for me again,
I put him in his place.

I remember, oh how I remember
The first girl that I kissed.
She was six and I was seven,
She was an angel sent from heaven.
We walked together hand in hand
Through bluebell'd woodland dells,
And when her hand touched mine
I thought that I heard bells.

Her cheeks were smooth as petals,
Her skin was soft as moss,
Her nose had tiny freckles
And her teeth were white as frost.
But her lips were warm as summer
And moist like morning mist, and
Slightly sticky from the sweets we
Swapped just before we kissed.

I remember I remember
Country walks come rain or shine,
Getting lost in spinneys and woods,
Losing track of time.
We sang with the birds,
We ran with the rabbits and hares,
Because the world they lived in
Was ours as much as theirs.

I remember I remember
We would listen to the wind moaning
And the trees wailing, the rain drumming
And the brook laughing,
And we would listen to the sound of silence
On high hills, when the afternoon world
Was lulled to a siesta of dandelion clocks
And buttercup chains.

I remember I remember
Digging up potatoes, for five bob a day,
Envying the other kids who just went out to play.
Scrumping apples from the orchard
For mum to make a pie,
Getting caught for stealing,
Being beaten 'til you cry.
But despite the deprivation, hard to say goodbye.

I remember I remember
When we let the old house down,
Packed our bags and boxes,
Moved to another town.
The willow tree was weeping,
The cold damp house was weeping too,
Tears trickled down the window panes
When I took a last walk through.

Alone, I quietly sang a sad song of goodbye
About a little white cloud that cried
And tears fell from the sky.
We left the fields, the woods, and freshwater stream,
And moved to a big city where I'd never been.
I knew my childhood ended then
And that my life, my world, would never,
Could never, be the same again.

I remember I remember
The new council house estate
Built for the working classes
With not much to celebrate.
But I missed the cold damp house,
I missed the tin bath too,
And I missed the ghost that lived
Outside in the backyard loo.

And now when I remember,
I remember I'm not fortune's fool.
Life is sometimes kind,
Sometimes life is cruel.
But with all that I may have lost,
And all that I've still got, I know now
Some things are worth remembering
And some are best forgot.

At RADA we were introduced to what was called *period technique*, i.e. Restoration Comedy. We were tutored in how to stand, walk, gesture, wear wigs and makeup, and seventeenth-century costume, and speak in the verse of that period. A whole new world. It was intriguing and great fun. So I was delighted in the early 1990s to be invited by the Royal Shakespeare Company to play Loveless in *The Relapse* by John Vanbrugh in London and at the Memorial Theatre in Stratford-upon-Avon. I have always loved being a member of a Company and it was a dream come true to be joining the RSC. I had already enjoyed playing some leading roles in the West End and at the National Theatre in London, but the RSC was something else, and top of my wish list.

Another great Shakespeare theatre company that I was lucky enough to work with is The Shakespeare Company in Washington, D.C., in America. So, in 2001, I was delighted to find myself in Washington as a member of this brilliant Company playing Horner in Wycherley's restoration comedy *The Country Wife*. The theatre was situated across town from Ford's Theatre, where President Abraham Lincoln was assassinated in 1865. He was shot by the actor John Wilkes Booth. I once had a theatrical agent in America who had a cautionary sign on his office desk that read *Don't forget Lincoln was shot by an actor*. About halfway through the run of *The Country Wife*, I was asked to play a leading role in Neil Simon's *Plaza Suite* for the Roundabout Theatre Company in New York City when I had finished in Washington. It would mean rehearsing *Plaza Suite* during the day and doing *The Country Wife* at matinées and evenings. A rather complicated rehearsal schedule was arranged, split between Washington and New York. Memorising, and retaining, two major theatrical roles in your head, in addition to travelling between Washington and New York for rehearsals, can make you feel like you are going insane, and some days you do just feel like shooting someone – anyone will do – it doesn't have to be a president!

I should have learnt my lesson earlier when, in the late 1990s, I found myself in a similar situation. I was in America playing the lead roles in two one-act plays called *Noël Coward in Two Keys* in a theatre in Sag Harbour, Long Island. The offer came through for me to return to the RSC in the UK immediately the Coward plays closed. The offer was to play Oberon and Theseus in Shakespeare's *A Midsummer Night's Dream*, with a request to know both parts by heart before rehearsals began at the RSC. It's not unusual for the same actor to play the two roles, as the characters never meet in the play, but learning both parts before you even start rehearsals is a formidable task. The very thought of holding four major roles in my head at the same time should have been enough to dissuade me from accepting and attempting such a feat. But like most actors, when offered a wonderful role – or in this case, four wonderful roles – I found reasons and excuses for me to accept and embark on a journey of terrifying proportions to the point where, for a time, I either was, or thought I was, going completely bonkers. My consolation prize? The following six months of playing Oberon and Theseus in England, Japan, Hong Kong, Australia, and New Zealand, was right up there as one of the most satisfying of my professional career. And why wouldn't it be? The privilege of speaking the words of the greatest poet that ever lived, six days a week, with the greatest Shakespeare Company in the world, is an experience to relish.

This poem, 'You and Me', was written for fun to represent a challenge for anyone to memorise. It took me weeks to finish, a bit like starting a very difficult jigsaw puzzle that I felt a compulsion to complete. It is also about things that go together, and opposites that attract. All the same, it is one I am very glad I do not have to memorise ...

You and Me

Sun and moon, dark and light, black and white,
    Day and night.
Ship and sail, boat and rudder, father, mother,
    Sister, brother.
Uncle and aunt, son and daughter, bricks and mortar,
    Fire and water.
Peace and love, below above, early and late,
    Destiny, fate.

Laugh and cry, wet and dry, can't and could,
    Shouldn't and should.
Hammer and nail, hill and dale, hot and cold,
    Young and old.
Hat and gloves, shoe and sock, praise and mock,
    Time and clock.
Sea and surf, cuss and curse, pen and ink,
    Kitchen and sink.

Begin and end, receive and send, needle and thread,
    Slumber and bed.
Up and down, city and town, arrive depart,
    Stop and start.
Apple and pear, ignore and stare, faith and prayer,
    Here and there.
Flesh and blood, sat and stood, sleep and wake,
    Mend and break.

Sex and drugs and rock and roll, rhythm and blues,
    Heart and soul.
Heaven and earth, death and birth, horse and cart,
    Meet and part.
Up and down, lost and found, short and long,
    Weak and strong.
Ever and never, sand and shore, rich and poor,
    Either, Or.

Ying and yang, tooth and fang, canvas and paint,
    'Tis and t'ain't.
Good and bad, happy and sad, old and grey,
    Go and stay.
Steeple and bell, buy and sell, right and wrong,
    Singer and song.
Come and go, yes and no, sorry and glad,
    Happy and sad.

Open and close, push and pull, empty and full,
    Cock and bull.
Tit for tat, this and that, here and there,
    Stallion and mare.
Sugar and spice, nasty, nice,
    Ink and pen, now and then.
Dogs and cats, houses and flats, sausage and mash,
    Beard, moustache.

King and crown, smile and frown, stocks and shares,
    Table and chairs.
Rhyme or reason, the four seasons, alive or dead,
    Garden shed.
When and where, here or there, dark or fair,
    Truth or dare.
House and home, Darby and Joan, rats and mice,
    Cut and splice.

Laugh or cry, live or die, low or high,
    Hello, goodbye.
Cruel and kind, lose and find, Milky Way,
    Leave or stay.
Give and take, tea and cake, buy and sell,
    Heaven and hell.
Stay and flee, land and sea, honey and bee,
    You and me.

After appearing in *The Merchant of Venice* on Broadway, I was offered some TV work in Hollywood. We moved to a lovely art deco house in Hancock Park, Los Angeles, and were very happy until a major earthquake put the fear of God into us. So we returned to the UK, and I started work playing the title role in a TV series called *Kinsey* for the BBC, shot mostly in Birmingham.

When we got back to the UK, I realised how much I had missed the seasons, even winter. In LA there are no real changes in the seasons; almost every day is a sunny day. Since then, I now look forward to each season in turn, and embrace the beauty of a rainy day, or a winter, snow-covered landscape, or an Indian Summer in autumn. It is on days like the one in this poem that endorse my desire to be in England when autumn comes ...

That Autumn Day

A carpet of brass and copper leaves rising and falling
As if the wood itself was breathing.
Red embers dripping from burning bushes
Join in ancient country dances.
A whispering wind pipes an autumn anthem.

Shards of cathedral light shaft through
Towering oaks, chestnut, and fir trees, majestic.
Leafy shadows dapple the sun's fingerprints
On yesterday's black trodden tracks,
Rippling in and out of time.

And that day on a toast-paved Monarch's Way,
Woodlands and wood lanes cornflake-crackle,
Threadbare hedgerows splattered marmalade-gold,
Honey-filled acorn cups and syrup-sap glisten.
And it was breakfast colours everywhere.

The Joseph tree, robbed by his evergreen
With envy brothers, sheds leaves like tears
From his canopy of many colours.
The soft sigh of the tree's lullaby,
The birds and summer going home.

And the cheeks of the evening sky blushed scarlet
Through the window over my quilted autumn bed.
Dear God, will there ever be another day like this,
When in Mother Nature's arms I'm held
And by her lips I'm goodnight kissed?

Laying on a beach in the sun can be blissful. But so can a winter's day when the roads, fields, meadows, and woods are blanketed with a thick layer of pure white snow ...

Winter White

That winter day was like skating on a cloud
    Through snow-white fairy-tale lands,
With tar-black trees silhouetted
    Against white, in a Bruegel winterscape.

Passing through hibernal washing powder lanes,
    Mother Nature's laundry flung everywhere,
Her children overdressed in the sameness of
    Showy, snowy whiteness
Until the season's Spring Collection is announced.

"It was such a spring day as breathes into a man an ineffable yearning, a painful sweetness, a longing that makes him stand motionless, looking at the leaves or grass, and fling out his arms to embrace he knows not what."
—John Galsworthy

"It is spring again. The earth is like a child that knows poems by heart."
—Rainer Maria Rilke

The First Day of Spring 2022

The river dawdles brown and foamy
Like undrunk frothy beer,
Two white swans
Bourrée en couru exquisitely,
Drifting near.

Wild-haired grasses,
Blow-dried by wind and sun,
Seek glamourous attention,
But here find none.

A meadow washed apple-green,
A sky of spilt-ink blue
Stains the spring landscape
That she and I walked through.

Bramble and hawthorn
Make spiteful grabs,
Sheep lay in shady shadow
Like scruffy knitted bags,

A woodpecker hammering a home
Above bog-soaked fallen trees.
Hot, hot, the electric sun,
Cool, cool, the ice cube breeze.

Then lost we were
In an enchanting wood
And lost there we would stay,
If only, if only we could.

I was appearing at the National Theatre in London in a new play by Peter Shaffer called *Yonadab*, with Sir Alan Bates and Sir Patrick Stewart, directed by Sir Peter Hall. When we took the play to Edinburgh, I caught pneumonia and had to recuperate in hospital and then fly home to rest for a few weeks.

One of London's rainy old days brought about this observation, and is one of the reasons I love the place whatever the weather, especially if you are cosy, warm, and dry at home, with a fire in the grate, and the radio playing ...

From the Balcony

Today. Today is a black and grey sort of day,
Clouds black and grey. Trees, leaves, and
White stucco houses around my way,
All black and grey today.

Streets grey, pavements grey, rooftops,
Chimneys, windows, blocks of flats,
Even dogs and cats,
All black and grey today.

Grey is the colour of the falling rain,
As it drips and drops into black iron drains.
Cars and lorries, wellies and brollies,
Blend and blur in the grey rain mist.

Lowry figures in mourning as the day dies.
The clouds part briefly,
The moon appears, but does not stay,
It's crescent-shaped and vapour-grey.

And as black night rests under its fleece,
Projects a profundity of evening peace,
Just as soon the day is old
And melts away, its story told.

Although I was born and spent my early years in Atherstone, Warwickshire, and both town and county will always hold a special place in my heart, I have lived most of my adult life in London, and was deeply honoured in 2017 to be made A Freeman of The City of London in an ancient ceremony in the beautiful and historic Guildhall building. My parents were bombed out of London during World War II and evacuated to Warwickshire in the Midlands. My mother was born and brought up in North London. My grandmother was born in the East End of London, within the sound of St Mary-le-Bow's church bells, which gave her the right to call herself a Cockney. When I was growing up in the middle of England, I used to dream of living in London. As soon as I was old enough, I packed my bags and headed for the capital, and have considered London as my home ever since.

More recently, many beautiful and historic buildings that miraculously escaped the Nazi bombing in World War II have since been demolished by greedy opportunists, and replaced with ugly, brutal, grotesque travesties. It breaks my heart to observe the current destruction of whole swathes of the city I love. London is in my blood – I feel a belonging. I feel an ownership.

During my acting career I have done a fair amount of filming in London. Shooting in some of the older, more historic, buildings and locations can still look stunningly beautiful, both live and on camera. However, the journey to and from the location in London these days can be a sad, depressing, and rather emotional experience due to the ruthless disrespect for our heritage by the demolition squads, architects, and construction companies, and lack of protection by those in power, who should know better:

"We shape our buildings and afterwards our buildings shape us."
—Winston Churchill

On a proposed new building in London:

"A monstrous carbuncle on the face of a much-loved and elegant friend."
—King Charles III

My London

Oh London. My London. Oh London, my city,
You used to be so pretty.

Now they have scarred your lovely face.
Concrete and glass in every conceivable place.
Demolished, destroyed, the features that made you great,
It's a cruel, irresponsible, irreversible fate.
Once a star who took first prize,
Your disfiguration touches all our lives.

Oh London. My London. Oh London, my city,
People from another place have squirted acid in your face.
The mighty buck, rouble, dinar and yen
Have savaged your beauty time and again.
No pride in, or respect for, your former glory.
They're rewriting the book, changing the story.

Proud Cockney Pearly King and Queen
Now rarely, if ever, seen.
Your kingdom lost and at what a cost.
Going, going, going – gone,
Without thought or reservation,
The symbols and treasures of a once proud nation.

Oh London. My London. Oh London, my city.
You used to be so pretty.

After World War II, even during the Blitz, the famous Windmill Theatre in London's West End proudly proclaimed *"we never closed"*. Before the war began, my mother was front of house manageress of this grand old venue, and she met my father there. He arrived in London from Glasgow with his male dance partner, as song and dance duo Lawson & Young, and appeared at the theatre until they were eventually bombed out of London by the Nazis. Many of the soldiers who volunteered for service at this time were just ordinary guys who, if they survived, were marked forever by the horrendous experiences they endured. I was brought up to respect these brave men and women. As mentioned, I was one of the first generation of Englishmen for many years who were not "called up" for National Service in the military on their eighteenth birthday.

This poem emerged on Remembrance Sunday 2018, when I was on a bus in London, and an old veteran got on proudly wearing a poppy in his beret, and his war medals across his chest ...

Albion

It was Remembrance Sunday, Poppy Day.
I was sitting on a bus
And I heard an old man say,
"I fought for my country you know,
We didn't want a war but we had to go.
We did it, we never dreamt of asking why,
We knew, of course, that some of us would die.
But we never questioned what we had to do,
We fought for our children and their children too.
We was proud then to be British,
Whether English, Irish, Welsh, or Scottish.
I think it's sad that some young'uns now
Don't respect the flag.
We thought at the time
The whole world's gone insane,
But nothing's changed much,
Hatred and war still remain.
I hope my mates didn't all die in vain."

Spending the second half of my childhood growing up on a council house estate called Tile Hill on the outskirts of Coventry, in Warwickshire, was not an altogether happy experience. I couldn't wait to leave school, get a job, and get out.

In 2014, many years later when I had, I suppose, found a certain amount of acceptance and identity as an actor, my wife and I were guests at the South Bank Sky Arts Awards ceremony in London. One of the nominees was the artist George Shaw, who had already been a runner-up for the Turner Prize three years or so earlier, and it was at that time I first became aware of his brilliant talent. George is more than twenty years younger than me, but was born and brought up about ten minutes away from my home on the same Tile Hill housing estate in Coventry. His incredible work has been hugely influenced by that background, and the Tile Hill estate features strongly in a lot of his work. When I got to know George a little, it came as no surprise how much he valued poetry in his creative journey as an artist. A recent Art and Literature exhibition at Christie's noted *"how the history of Art and Literature are inextricably linked. An ancient epic poem could inspire an old master painting; a contemporary artist takes flight from a Shakespearean phrase; a medieval illuminated manuscript combines text and painting in a single beautiful object. At times direct and at other times more subtly and allusively expressed. The creative partnership between art and literature has been intertwined for thousands of years."*

I was blown away when I first saw George Shaw's superbly realised paintings of the housing estate where we had both grown up. When I met him at the South Bank Awards, I told him so. I also told him I had written a poem in tribute to his work and the parallels in our lives. I recited a couple of verses from this poem, and he tells me he now has the copy I later gave him, framed, and hanging in his studio, and I treasure the painting he gave me that he painted of Berkswell churchyard. Berkswell churchyard is mentioned in my poem, before I even knew it was somewhere as a young boy that George also loved to escape to on his bicycle ...

Backward Glances
(Ode to George Shaw)

Two Warwickshire lads, two Coventry kids,
Decades apart on time's grid,
Journeyed away from what was back in the day
As ugly, as brutal, savage and bleak
As many another council estate street.

Both had visions. Both had dreams.
Does the future have to be as desolate as it seems?
Do prospects have to appear so hopeless and absurd?
One created pictures with paint.
The other painted pictures with words.

George Shaw, you could have,
Should have, been my mate
Before I learned to act,
Before you learned to paint,
And prove it isn't so absurd,
You can change your life
With the paintbrush or the word.

I could have, should have, known George.
He could have, should have, known me,
On that housing estate in Coventry.
We would have, perhaps, should have, perhaps,
Strolled the pavements of your paintings together,
Entering and exiting streets next door to one another.

Or would we have been in rival street gangs,
Running wild through enemy lands,
Pockets full of ammunition, searching for cover
From lads throwing stones
And insults at each other?

Did you, as did I, frantic-peddle on your bike
Till council estate no longer in sight?
Freedom. Escape from the gangs and warfare
On that vile hill, that "Tile Hill"
Council estate.

Did you, as did I, find no redeeming feature,
No kindly caring teacher at the concrete school
Where bullies rule?
Peddling till legs shaking,
Escaping to a happier destination.

On. On. To Berkswell village church,
Where peace, tranquillity, and ghosts inside lurk
In the bare stone nave and prayer-sodden pews,
Stained glass windows and *The Parish News*,
Six centuries of lives in graveyard tombs.

The irony that your art could now bring me pleasure,
Mementos of bleak times I begrudgingly treasure.
Can nostalgia bear witness to society's sickness?
To despair and discontent,
To a childhood misspent?

The very beauty of your art
Transcends the ugliness of that brutal start,
A canvas of such exquisite perfection
Challenges my childish recollection
With visions of such wonder,
My turgid grief is blown asunder.

Backward glances perceived in a different way
Now bounce off walls in the West End and Broadway,
The Turner Prize, The National Gallery,
Movies, books, TV, the RA and the Tate,
Formed in embryo on that council estate.
Paint and brush. Prosody and words.
Not now so hopeless. Not now so absurd.

The famous eighteenth-century actor, writer, and poet, David Garrick is one of only a few actors buried in Poet's Corner in Westminster Abbey, where many of the Monarchs of England were once interred. Garrick is reputed to have said about an actor's life *"our names are writ in water"*, although the poet John Keats immortalised similar words on his grave-stone in Rome some years later. Another actor buried in Westminster Abbey is Sir Henry Irving, the first theatrical knight, who died in 1905. In 1871, on the opening night of the play *The Bells*, Irving's first major success, Irving was accompanied in his carriage from the theatre by his young wife of two years, who said to him, *"Are you going on making a fool of yourself like this all your life?"* Irving halted the coachman, exited their carriage, and walked off into the night, and chose never to see her again. In 1905, when he was appearing on stage as Becket, he suffered a stroke just after uttering Becket's dying words *"Into thy hands, O Lord, into thy hands"*, and never spoke again. He died an hour later. A more recent actor to be honoured with a burial in Westminster Abbey is the late, great, Laurence Olivier. I think it was Olivier who said *"films for money, television for fame, but the proper place for an actor is in the theatre."*

Unfortunately, as one gets older, attending funerals starts to become a more frequent event. St Paul's Church in London's Convent Garden district is known as "The Actor's Church", and I have said goodbye to a few dear friends there over the years with varying degrees of sadness and loss, and it is, I suppose, where I'll end up also. I used to see most friends and fellow actors, or members of the theatrical club, at awards ceremonies, premiers, or first nights; it seems funerals have now taken over. To be honest, I quite like a nice funeral – but I'm not quite ready for my own yet! I personally have no desire to follow in the footsteps of Henry Irving, or for that matter of my great-great aunt, the much-loved music hall/vaudeville star, Marie Lloyd. She also died on stage with the sound of her audience's laughter echoing in her ears, thinking that her staggering and falling to the boards was a part of her act, until the curtain was brought in and an announcement was made that the great lady had died.

This poem was written upon my receiving the news from his much younger wife, that a rather posh, and a bit pompous, heavy-drinking old thespian, that I didn't actually know, had taken his final curtain ...

That Time of Year

I didn't die of the wine M'dear,
I didn't die of the beer.
I died because it was time M'dear,
It was just that time of year.

I didn't die of smoking M'dear,
The tobacco or the weed.
I didn't die of a wicked act
Or for that matter of good deed.

I didn't die because I deserved it M'dear,
Through anger, spite or fear.
I died because it was time M'dear,
It was just that time of year.

This poem was written and read by me at my dear friend Sebastian Graham Jones's funeral. Sebastian was an actor, musician, theatre and TV director, who died far too early. He directed my first TV series, *Travelling Man*, in England in the 1980s. His girlfriend, Susan Fleetwood, who also appeared in the series, was a wonderful actress and sister of Mick Fleetwood of the band Fleetwood Mac. Susan also died tragically young a few years before Sebastian. Sebastian's best friend, Duncan Brown, was a very gifted musician and composer, who wrote the music for *Travelling Man* that played to 18million people every week on UK TV. Duncan's music became very popular, once or twice entering the hit parade. Duncan died a few years before Sebastian, also far too young. I sometimes wonder if Sebastian found this world all just too much, and decided to go and join them in the next.

I loved Seb, and I miss them all still ...

The Hollow Space

A hollow space
    At my table in his place.
I hoped we would grow old
    Or older together.
He in me, must now live forever.

True and loyal beyond belief
    Like a brother now shrouds in grief.
A look, a laugh, a clever remark,
    A kindness, uncommon generosity
All from him – now mine to be.

Never erased. Written indelible.
    Too, too early taken.
Too unbearable.
    But think on this, on this think on,
Ever with me here, never truly gone.

Written when my long-time, very dear friend, Mike King passed away. Mike, along with his two brothers, made up a very popular trio in the early sixties known as The King Brothers. Mike was married to the actress Carole White, who played the lead in the groundbreaking Ken Loach film *Cathy Come Home*. She broke Mike's heart when she left him for Frank Sinatra, who dumped her after a brief affair.

I was lucky enough to have Mike as a friend for about forty years, and never heard him say a cruel thing about anyone. My life would have been very different and not nearly such fun without Mike in it. I miss him, and his laughter ...

Adios

Adios amigo,
  Cheerio old friend,
I'll see you on the other side
  When the journey ends.

We took the trail less travelled,
  Met some like minds along the way,
Some moved on without us,
  A few decided to stay.

Our garden of friendship was well tended
  And nurtured with laughter and wine.
I still walk there and remember
  Now and then, from time to time.

You. Who were always there.
  You. Who always had the time.
Now I'll tread the road alone.
  Goodbye dear friend of mine.

Someone once remarked that a book is in some aspects like a box – you open it and delve into it to discover its contents.

I was filming the movie *Sword of the Valiant* in Ireland when 'Safely Stowed' appeared one day, after viewing at an auction house in Dublin. Whilst there I came across an old wooden box, inside was a black leather-bound prayer book, inside the book was a pressed, faded, red rose. And for some reason it reminded me of these lines from the poem 'To His Coy Mistress' by the seventeenth-century poet Andrew Marvell:

> *"And your quaint Honour turn to dust;*
> *And into ashes all my Lust.*
> *The Grave's a fine and private place,*
> *But none I think do there embrace."*

Safely Stowed

And now your secrets are safely hid,
    Safe with you inside a
Book cover coffin lid,
    All that was said, all that was hid.

And now even your quiescent mind
    Can no longer be read,
Because memories lie dormant
    In the vast library of the dead.

A worn, black prayer book,
    A pressed, faded rose,
Should tell some sort of story
    Of lost love, I suppose.

When I was initially offered the leading role in my first TV series, *Travelling Man*, I hesitated to accept the offer. It was a wonderful part, a very good script, a handsome fee, and a six-month shoot in the UK. So why did I hesitate? Fame! That's why. Television makes you famous – almost instantly – and when you are appearing on the television regularly you are also in danger of becoming public property. Everywhere you go you are recognised, and people start to behave strangely, differently, both people you already know and perfect strangers. People you have never met assume they know you. I had seen this happen to other actor friends and people I worked with. I didn't become an actor to become famous, I became an actor because I love, and am passionate about, acting. I had already had enough trouble handling the little bit of fame that had been forced upon me so far in my career. I think the experience of fame sort of alarmed me – it felt too loose, too out of my control, and too fragile and transient to trust.

When my agent enquired as to why I was hesitating in accepting the offer of *Travelling Man*, I explained my apprehensions and reservations about entering that arena. His response was *"You have chosen the wrong profession to remain anonymous!"* In retrospect, I think I may also have been a little afraid of fame, and nervous and uncertain of the responsibilities and consequences that come with it as an inevitable part of the deal. One aspect of my concern was further confirmed in 2005 when I played the role of stepfather to Casanova in the film of that name, played by Heath Ledger. Heath was a lovely guy and a very talented young actor. He died of an accidental overdose of drugs around a year after the film was released. I believe that Heath, like so many others, also found fame hard to deal with – and prescription drugs were his escape.

So anyway, I did the TV series and became a well-known, recognisable face for a time – I didn't like it ...

"When you're a young actor you run to success, which also includes fame. And the minute you get there you can get burnt good. Everything gets elevated in terms of what you can do or say – you have to learn how to be responsible. I'm lucky I got famous when I was 33, not 23. I'd have been shooting crack into my forehead if I had been 23 and given money and success."
—George Clooney, *Sunday Times Culture magazine, November 2021*

The Suit

He was given a suit to wear,
Bought from a shop called Fame.
The label said once worn
Your life would never be the same.

He tried the suit on and wore it once or twice,
But it wasn't very comfortable, it wasn't very nice,
It didn't really suit him or fit him very well
And he didn't like the colour or the material.

The suit was rather garish and loud
And seemed to attract the wrong sort of crowd,
It signalled to others the unwanted impression
They could interrupt his life on any occasion.

Walking down a street, in a restaurant or bar,
Even standing at a urinal or getting out of a car,
People felt compelled to speak to him, called him a star,
It was alien, strange, weird, and bizarre.

"You're that actor, aren't you? When you on TV again?"
Autographs and selfies no matter where or when,
Paparazzi stalked him, waited outside his door.
He craved the life he lost. He couldn't bear it anymore.

So that suit was disregarded, that suit was put aside,
Till all the fuss calmed down, and all the fame thing died.
Then that suit was thrown away,
And he's happily back in denim shirt and jeans today.

Someone once said, *"Fame rarely provides the answers that those seeking it expect to find."*

Fame is a double-edged sword. It makes some people happy to be famous. It destroys others. Some just put up with it. Some enjoy it. But fame comes at a price, and can in itself be a dangerous commodity. Seeking fame for fame's sake is a precarious pursuit.

There are, of course, degrees of fame, and it affects different people in different ways. Some not always for the better ...

Fame

So now you've got what you wanted,
Your dreams have all come true,
You're famous, you're a star,
Wherever you go people know who you are.

So now star of stage and screen
Say goodbye to what might have been.
You're the cat that got the cream.
You're the one living the dream.

How sweet you were before... before...
Why don't you trust your friends anymore?
Now we are strangers at your door,
Be careful, my lovely, who you open it for.

Someone once gave this advice:
Fame is attractive, but first check the price.
The desire for fame knows no cure
And can eat at your soul like a soporific sore.

Fame needs feeding, it's a drug,
It dissolves the need for any other love.
Fame, like cocaine, wants more and more.
I've seen people addicted to both before.

You say you love and need me still
And that's what friends are for.
But you know what my beauty?
I'm really... it's... I'm no longer sure.

In 1977 I was invited to play a role in a movie called *Golden Rendezvous*, to be shot in South Africa. I was told I would be needed for six weeks, but was there for over three months. It was a miserable experience for the most part in that beautiful, unsettled, and deeply disturbed country.

Given that one might safely assume that no one actually sets out to make a bad movie, it's quite staggering how many bad movies are released. Although I cannot claim ultimate responsibility for the final product, I have to confess I have been in a few clangers myself – and this was one of them. Who knew? *Golden Rendezvous* had some tasty ingredients in its recipe. It was based on a successful book by the well-respected writer, Alistair Maclean. It had a generous budget. It had some heavy duty, well known British and American actors: Richard Harris, Burgess Meredith, John Carradine, David Janssen, Dorothy Malone, Gordon Jackson, and Christopher Lee, amongst others. I got on very well with Richard Harris, who was playing the lead, and I liked him and his then girlfriend, Ann Turkel, who was also in the movie. I felt honoured to meet a few of the old-timers that I remembered from movies when I was a young boy. But *Golden Rendezvous* was not a happy rendezvous. At one point the film crew were close to mutiny. Richard was not happy with the script and attempted, not very successfully, to rewrite it. Actors were sacked and new ones brought in. Something would go catastrophically wrong almost every day. I began to wish I were one of the lucky actors, like Christopher Lee, who were replaced – but no such luck. I had to stay to the bitter, and I mean bitter, end. When I eventually got back home to the UK, I told my agent, *"No more movies – I want to concentrate on my true love, and the reason I became an actor in the first place – and that was to work in the theatre."* Anyway, I had made a pact with myself to try and never leave it much more than a year or so before returning to the theatre. So that is exactly what I did – for a year – until a leading part of Alec d'Urberville in a movie called *Tess* came along.

Despite the unfortunate *Golden Rendezvous* experience, there is no doubt that it was great to be around in the 1960s and through the 1970s. There is also no doubt that to be young at that time was even better, and to be young in London better still. Young people were gaining a voice in the world, new exciting music was emerging, and a revolution was evolving in what was possible for young, working class, people to achieve. A revolution in the way we dressed, how we thought, how we behaved. For the first time, fashion, music, art, was being dictated by "the street", not couture houses, studios, or galleries. As well as The Beatles, we had the Liverpool poets, like McGough, Patten, Henri, amongst others in the UK, who had been influenced by the earlier Beat Poets, led by Ginsberg and Kerouac in America, who were introducing a new much freer, more accessible form of poetry, bringing fun and irreverence to the process. The Hippie movement of flower power, love and peace, had taken hold in the UK, America, and beyond. Psychedelia also played a major part in what was happening. Art and music reflected the influence of altered states as a result of psychedelic drugs such as LSD, mescaline, psilocybin, and marijuana.

During one of the interminably empty weeks in beautiful South Africa, waiting to be recalled for shooting on *Golden Rendezvous*, I received a letter from a friend in England who had cleverly concealed a tab of LSD on a small piece of blotting paper under the stamp on the envelope. I waited until I had enough time to spend a few days travelling through a breathtakingly beautiful area known as "The Garden Route" to drop the tab of acid. It was a wonderful spectacular trip in every way; the landscape, the moon, the stars, especially the evening light, were all spectacularly unworldly. Some thoughts and poems had emerged on the back of my film script, which I took with me, when I returned to the location. I think this poem appeared at around that time, and was definitely influenced by The Beatles' song 'Lucy in the Sky with Diamonds' ...

Tripping. The Light. Fantastic.

Who will burn with the glowworms
And I the midnight oil?
Who will fly with the sky fish
To visit the grateful dead
To give thanks for life,
Gratefully living it to death?

Dreaming in Slumber Street,
Sauntering down Sweet Dream Lane,
On either side powder-blue fir trees,
Golden-red grasses whispering secret messages,
Trees barking out time rings,
But you've learned not to hear.

Gypsy leaves, brown and ragged travelling
On the highway of dreams.
Blackbirds singing centuries-old country songs,
Scarlet flying pigeon birds, electric peacocks
With kaleidoscope fantailed strut.
Gold-rimmed purple rain clouds.

We'll bribe pink-eyed white mice to eat sugar people.
We'll let them lead us to the beach of sapphire sand,
Lapped by the milk-white sea.
We'll wear gifts from vampire birds, emerald green and
Primrose-yellow silk gowns, with foxgloves and
Bluebells ringing.

Let's fall on black fur lawns,
Let's shout songs at a crooked sky,
Let's spread love and peace before we die,
Let's do foolish things like Solomon
So that people think we're wise.
Let's look and see the universe in each other's eyes.

Upon returning to England, after three months in South Africa filming *Golden Rendezvous*, I was rewarded and thrilled to be cast as Yasha in Anton Chekov's masterpiece *The Cherry Orchard*. Directed by the brilliant Peter Gill, it was to mark the opening of Riverside Studios in London. The play turned out to be a landmark production that I felt privileged to be part of. I could hardly wait for morning to arrive so that I could get to rehearsals; in fact, I would sometimes go to rehearsals even if I was not called that day, just to be there and not miss a moment. Shortly after we had given our last performance my agent rang to say I had been offered one of the lead parts of Alec d'Urberville in the movie *Tess*, based on Thomas Hardy's *Tess of the d'Urbervilles*. No interview, no screen test, just a straight offer. I reminded my agent that I was not interested in doing any more movies and wanted to concentrate on the theatre, and asked him to tell them thank you very much and turn the part down. A week later they came back and asked me to reconsider. I said no. Two weeks later they came back again. This time my agent convinced me that I should do the movie, and I'm so glad that his good sense prevailed. I spent a year in France shooting *Tess*, the film was directed by Roman Polanski, again co-starring one of my best friends, Peter Firth, as Angel Clare, and Nastasia Kinsky, one of the most beautiful women in the world, as Tess. What's not to like? Well, quite a lot as it turned out – although also quite a lot to enjoy, but that's a whole other story, and a whole other year of my life, and I wouldn't have missed it for the world.

When *Tess* was released, I was asked to do some promotion. The film was being released worldwide, and was nominated for six Academy Awards, and won three. It also won two Golden Globe Awards, a British Academy Award, and three Cesar Awards in France. Promotion involved countless press and TV interviews in America, Canada, Australia, France, Belgium, and Holland, amongst others. I returned to England after completing the tour to do more publicity in the UK.

A technique or strategy used by the more unscrupulous members of the British journalistic profession is to request an in-depth interview about your work, career, and projects you are currently working on. A lunch at an expensive restaurant is then suggested to further flatter your ego, and in the hope that the expensive wine will loosen your tongue. After an hour or so of feigned interest in your work and aspirations, questions about your private life and loves start to creep into the conversation. When the interview finally appears in the newspapers it contains very little, if anything, about the passion you have for your work, and is instead centred almost entirely on the passions of your private life and loves that you didn't want to, and should not have, talked about in the first place.

You have been duped and the journalist has earned his thirty pieces of silver ...

The Interview

He plied me with food and fine wine,
The better to steal my precious time,
Pretended to be interested in my career,
But it cost me dear, to bend his ear.

He was in the Business known as Show,
And I? I was a naïve young fool to go.
Next Sunday morning at the news stall
A poster stood proclaiming all.

My private pain for all the world to see,
And my picture in the newspaper
Starring back at me.
I learned a lesson on that day.

Caution is the only way.
Draw a line between what you think
And what you say
Or you may well live to rue the day.

I mentioned earlier that in 1974 I found myself in India, appearing in a movie called *Ghost Story*, directed by Stephen Weeks; the first of two movies I was to make with him. Stephen put together a wonderful cast of British actors, including Murray Melvin, Penelope Keith, and Marianne Faithfull. Marianne, her companion, and I travelled out to India together from the UK. When we arrived in Delhi, I continued on to Mysore to commence filming. I was told Marianne and her companion decided to spend a couple of days trying out some opium dens in Delhi. We shot a lot of the film, and also lived, in the decaying splendour of the Maharaja of Mysore's palace. I believe *Ghost Story* was shown at the Sitges Film Festival. One of the judges on the panel was the film director Roman Polanski, who later cast me as Alec D'Urberville in his film *Tess*. Work finds work!

We made *Ghost Story* on a Favoured Nations Agreement, which in this instance meant a reduction in upfront fees for a share of the profit. When we eventually got paid, Stephen bought a small castle on the Welsh border to live in. I bought a 400-year-old house in Mallorca, Spain, to escape to.

I loved my house in Mallorca and had many happy years there. Spring comes early in Mallorca; by February, thousands of almond trees blossom, and the island is a breathtaking kaleidoscope of white, pink, red, and purple. In the summer we would sleep on the roof terrace. You could see every star in the Milky Way, and there were always so many shooting stars to make a wish upon that we would often run out of wishes before falling asleep – better than an opium den. Although I have to admit that at the time I was more than a little disappointed to miss the opportunity to visit an opium den with Marianne Faithfull. To have been able to make that claim would have increased my social standing and street cred considerably!

Summer Streets
(Mallorca)

You could taste the air on that summer's day
    Beneath almond trees and fountains,
And just beyond the little town,
    The painted purple mountains.
Rising, rippling, mirage heat
    In the village square where lovers meet
Caught our breath and burnt our cheeks
    And scorched our lips and fingertips,
In those ancient dusty streets.
    Still no better place on earth to be.
Sun, heat, dust, you, me.

Not sure what I was smoking when this first appeared! It was the 1970s after all, and I was shooting a commercial in Jamaica – where the sea was very blue, the sun was very hot, the rum was very strong, and the ganja was very potent ...

Auscultation

Living inside a stereophonic sound
    Pushing sonorescence through my mind,
Reciting a sonic sonnet for the sadmad
    In the asylum for the sane.

One of the sadmad was heard to say
    Is there any rumour in the truth?
And was answered by the man
    With no face, who turned to say,

Oh yes, there is much rumour in the truth
    But it's falling. Pull, pull it up, young man,
Pull by whatever means you can.
    Knowing well that it was no use

Because he couldn't climb out anyway,
    But stood watchthinking
That's as far as the truth and rumour go.
    But a promise did make to the sadmad:

I will give an eternity to you.
    I will give a hundred thousand years to you,
From me; for friends we have been together,
    And time, like loneliness, goes on forever.

When I was a young actor, smoking and boozing quite heavily appeared to be the norm among my group of friends. Actors we admired and therefore tried to emulate, such as Peter O'Toole, Richard Harris, Richard Burton, Albert Finney, etc, were also famous for being big drinkers and "hellraisers", as they were called. This sounded fun, so we rather stupidly followed their example I suppose.

I never thought I would, or could, stop smoking. I never thought I would, or could, stop drinking. I stopped smoking after doing the play *Yonadab* at the National Theatre in London. Towards the end of the play I was required to lay on the stage completely naked and covered in a freezing cold concoction of a mud-like substance every matinée and evening performance. Not surprisingly, halfway through the run I contracted pneumonia. I had to have several weeks off to recover and followed my doctor's advice to stop smoking during that time.

I went to Morocco in 2015 to join Rebecca Ferguson and Iain Glenn, to appear in an American mini-series called *The Red Tent*, which was being shot there. We were shooting mostly in the Sahara Desert. The day I got back to the UK an American actor friend, Bobby Cannavale, came to visit. We had a quiet dinner at home and quite a lot of wine to celebrate my return. After dinner I began to feel unwell and had to go to bed to lie down. Shortly, I began to have violent tremors and convulsions, was rushed to Chelsea and Westminster Hospital, and put into the intensive care unit where it was discovered I had contracted E. coli in Morocco; they thought I was dying. I thought I was dying. At times I felt so ill I wished I was dying. Although there was no direct connection to the booze, when I returned home I decided to stop drinking and this poem appeared ...

No More Wineing

Rise from bed,
    Clear head,
Early not late,
    Feel great,
Finish breakfast,
    None left over,
Don't need coffee,
    No hangover.

Go for a walk,
    Spring in step,
Looking good,
    Johnny Depp.
Lunch on time,
    Water not wine,
Dinner the same,
    Ahead of the game.

Tomorrow do it all again,
    Thank you God,
Sweet dreams.
    Amen.

Whilst appearing in *The Merchant of Venice* with Dustin Hoffman, Dustin and I would sometimes discuss our shared passion for the theatre and acting, and why we chose it as a profession. After much discussion we finally arrived at the conclusion that *"you don't choose it, it chooses you"*. My son chose (or was chosen) to live a life in the theatre and became a very talented director and teacher, and obtained a Master's Degree in Theatre Studies. I am very proud of him.

Before my first grandson was born someone told me, *"You don't know what real love is until you have a grandchild."* True or not, the immense and overwhelming impact of welcoming my grandson onto the world stage had a profound effect on this old thespian. Will he be the fourth generation born and blessed (some may say cursed) with the performing gene?

It's a mystery what triggers the birth of a poem. The creative process is often motivated by extremes of emotion. This poem was born shortly after my first grandson, Solomon, and the emotion was just as powerful when Jackson came along four years later ...

This Boy

He gives me joy. This boy.
Unspeakable. Inexpressible.
This boy gives me joy.
Ineffable. Unexplainable.
This boy brings me joy.

Let bells ring. Choirs sing.
Chimes chime. Poets rhyme.
Trumpets trump. Drums drum.
Feet stamp. Guitars strum.

Higher than the moon,
Oh, hotter than the sun,
Deeper than the sea,
Is the joy this boy brings to me.

In 1991, after completing a successful year and a very enjoyable run playing Antonio in *The Merchant of Venice*, I was invited to LA to play the title role in a TV pilot called *The Dark Avenger*. I had been to Hollywood before but I had not actually filmed there. Following that I was offered a role in a TV mini-series with Jessica Lange and Anne Heche, called *O Pioneers!*, adapted from the novel by Willa Cather. It was all to be shot in the state of Nebraska. On the first day of filming when I arrived at the location for hair, makeup, and costume, everyone had a huge smile on their faces and looked very happy indeed. When I entered the makeup trailer I realised why – the air reeked of marijuana. The crew had bunches of weed protruding from every pocket, bags of it were scattered every-where, even the microwave oven was bulging with the stuff for some reason. When I enquired what was going on, I was gleefully informed that this part of Nebraska used to cultivate hemp plants to be made into rope, and that it still grows wild along the roadside and in many of the surrounding fields where the cattle graze. Maybe that's why even the cows seemed to have a smile on their faces. Apparently, they can't control the hemp from growing, or get rid of the stuff. It was there one evening that I came across a piece about the not so happy life and death of a man in the local newspaper. Before long this ode to Jonathan Nunn came into being ...

Jonathan Nunn

Jonathan Nunn
He had no Dad, he had no Mum.
Jonathan Nunn
Was on the run from things past,
From things to come,
Jonathan Nunn.

John Nunn
Hid in corners.
Hid from himself, hid from everyone.
John Nunn
Liked being sad. Hated fun,
John Nunn.

Johnny John Nunn
Didn't want friends and he had none.
Johnny John Nunn
Hated the sun, liked the dark,
And longed for night to come,
Johnny John Nunn.

John, John Nunn
Likes to booze, but don't like food,
Not even a crumb.
John, John Nunn
Gets drunk when he can on bottles of rum
Does Johnny, John Nunn.

J.J. Nunn
When he was younger,
Was a bare-knuckle fighter
With a strong left hook
And a lethal righter,
Said some of J.J. Nunn.

Johnny Nunn
Sometime later stole a gun,
Filled it with lead, shot himself in the head.
They found him in the neighbourhood
Lying dead in a pool of blood.
Johnny, John Nunn.

A man from the Fed said he was glad
Johnny was dead.
"Born a bum, died a bum,"
That's what he said,
The man from the Fed about
Johnny Nunn.

Johnny John Jonathan Nunn
Born a slave, died a bum.
Born and died no man's son.
Never took and never gave.
Lying now in an unmarked grave.
Never believed in better to come. In a life to come,
Not Johnny, not John, not J.J., not Jonathan Nunn.

Leaving a message in the form of a piece of poetry for a loved one can be something that lives on after you are no longer around. In this case, my grandchildren, Solomon, Joni, Evelina, Jackson, and Theo ...

Tick Tock

The drip, drip, drop of eternity,
The tick, tick, tock of time,
The ubiquitous universe of nothingness,
The vast expanse of mind.

The first note that ends in a symphony,
The first stone that becomes a tower,
The first step that leads to a mile,
The tiny seed that grows to a flower.

The cornerstone that evolves to a colossus,
An acorn that creates a forest,
A first drop of rain before a storm descends,
For each and every, a beginning and an end.

The power of a dream to transcend,
The boundaries that others impose,
To finish the story you started
Before your book is closed.

And you, my newborn love,
All the above transcend,
And give to my book of life a completeness
That only God can send.

I had fallen in love with Sussex, on the South Coast of England, whilst appearing at the Chichester Festival Theatre in a six-and-a-half-hour adaptation of Charles Dickens's novel, *Nicholas Nickleby*. I was playing the evil Uncle Ralph. The production was brilliantly directed by Jonathan Church and Philip Franks. However, six and a half hours a day on stage on matinée days, despite an also brilliant company, was overkill, and after each performance I would say to myself, *"I must remember never to do this again."* So I reluctantly decided not to continue when the show transferred to the West End and then on to Toronto in Canada. I was sad to leave this wonderful cast. But I was well represented by my talented son, Ace, who took on the responsibilities of Assistant Director for the rest of the run.

Church House has been in existence since 1670. It stands opposite a twelfth-century church, near the south coast of Sussex, a few minutes from Chichester. We bought and moved into Church House three days before the first Covid lockdown in 2020 …

Church House

And did I in another life lived
Sit in this very garden,
Gaze at the old church tower,
Or re-born here and now this hour?

And could your ancient stones speak,
What stories would they tell,
Reaching from earth to heaven,
From grave to tower bell?

Five hundred years
Of joy, of sorrow,
Of yesterdays lived,
Of hopes for the morrow.

Oh, teach me then old stones
How to grow old with your grace,
How to age with dignity through time
As life moves on apace.

I admire the artist Grayson Perry; he has an enormous appetite for life, great talent, and is a force to be reckoned with. I first met him over forty years ago when he was the "tea boy" where I got my hair cut. He was knighted in King Charles's New Year's Honours list 2023. In 2017 he invited my wife and I to the Royal Academy Summer Exhibition in Piccadilly, London. Grayson is himself a work of art. His frock and make-up that day put all others at the exhibition in the shade, and when he smiled it lit up the overcrowded room. We didn't find a painting there that we wanted to buy, but there was a chair in the corner of one of the rooms that caught my eye ...

The Chair at the Royal Academy Summer Exhibition

I have supported with sturdy legs
And welcomed with open arms
Many a weary traveller
Who passed my way and fell for my charms.

Always susceptible to flattery,
Many and varied derrières have mounted me.
"Ah that's better," I've heard them say,
Then they just get up and walk away.

I had never seen them live, despite being friends with some of the band for several years. In 2018, one of the band arranged some tickets for us for their London concert at Twickenham Stadium. The tickets were for places in the VIP area, at the very front of the stage and catwalk that extended out into the packed stadium. The band were beyond sensational, each a star in their own right. I was completely blown away by these guys, now in their seventies, but having lost none of their phenomenal magic, charisma, and danger. There are some pretty obvious clues in the title and verses of this poem as to who the band are ...

Jumping Jack Flash

I saw them once, up on the stage,
Veteran minstrels of indeterminate age.
Gathering no moss, with proverbial name,
They did that fevered congregation claim.

Owning the boards with pose and swagger,
Exceeding expectation and truly stagger.
A hundred-thousand pairs of eyes
Felt their gaze and took home their prize.

Cavorting, strutting, jumping like Jack Flash,
Old guitar whine and vintage drum bash.
They sang my life and history
In that vast arena for only me.

They sang their life too,
on that day, in that place,
Every note, every line, etched
Like a map on each famous face.

Filling in honeycombs of empty spaces,
That love, and hope, and dreams,
Lost in decades now dead,
Were once by them created.

Despite a couple of previously mentioned, self-inflicted, masochistic safaris of brain-busting proportions in attempting to memorise four major roles at the same time, I have been blessed with something of a photographic memory, and have mostly been able to learn pages of dialogue in a relatively short time. Despite this, some writers are easier to memorise than others.

In 2008 I played Messerschmann in a production of the Jean Anouilh play *Ring Around the Moon* at the Playhouse Theatre in London's West End, directed by the talented Sean Mathias. I had worked with Sean previously at the Soho Theatre in London, on a play called *Shoreditch Madonna*, written by the gifted writer Rebecca Lenkiewicz. Sean has an unerring instinct for theatre; he knows what works and what doesn't. In the Anouilh play my character had a speech containing a whole list of unconnected commodities – it was a nightmare to memorise, and fell flat every time at previews. I just wanted to cut it from the script. The director kept giving me a note to go faster and faster with the list. One night, early in the run, I managed to follow his advice and galloped at breakneck speed through it. Upon finishing, and to my complete surprise, it got a huge laugh and spontaneous round of applause!

My dear departed mate, the actor Bob Hoskins, told me he had a similar experience when doing a play with Sir John Gielgud. Bob asked Sir John how to deal with a particularly tricky dead line he had to deliver in the play they were doing together, Gielgud told Bob, *"Dear boy, take one pace forward – pause – and then say the line."* Next night, Bob took a pace forward, paused, said the line, and got a huge laugh! Bob said he tried it later in other plays, with other lines, to no effect whatsoever! Ah, the art and mysteries of playing comedy. The celebrated nineteenth-century actor Edmund Kean reputedly groaned on his death bed *"dying is easy – comedy is hard."* Who knows? Did he mean acting the two experiences? Or experiencing them first hand himself?

I have no idea how it happened, but I seem to be eighty-one years old! Is it time to retire? Do actors retire? Should actors retire? Can actors retire? It is over fifty years since the first poem in this little book was written. I have not acted for some while, whilst becoming preoccupied and distracted by other commitments and endeavours, compiling this book amongst them. Out of the blue, I recently received a movie script and was offered an interesting role to play in a film being made in Prague. The real problem is, although acting can sometimes be torture, and a burdensome compulsion, I have never lost my passion for my profession. Now, as I approach my eighty-second year, most of which have been spent practising my craft, the passion remains. Offers of work become less frequent, and the physical demands increase as one gets older. But, as I glance at the script which now lies on my desk staring back at me, challenging me to learn and make those words my own – or rather my characters – I face the ever-recurring dilemma: shall I accept the role, pack my bags, and poetry anthology, make my way to Prague, do the movie, and hope the experience is a good one, and worthwhile? And who knows, when I return home, maybe a poem will have appeared on the back page of my script, perhaps entitled 'Swan Song' ...

The Glory Days

The glory days on stage
Are most behind him now.
First night fears, last night tears,
Have taken a final bow.

The theatre, the plays,
The critics, the praise,
The camaraderie backstage,
Those were the glory days.

An evening spent as someone else.
Here and now, before and after.
Drawing tears or provoking laughter.
Those were the glory days.

The slog of learning pages by heart,
The joy of playing a marvellous part,
Dinner with friends after the show.
Could he ever let this go?

A proscenium arch, well-trodden boards,
The overture and beginners, opening chords.
Final curtain, cheers, applause,
Those were the glory days.

So, is it goodbye for ever and ever?
Or is it a matter of never say never?

I think about death quite a lot, not in a morbid way, but as an inevitability. I hear a piece of music, or read a poem, and think that would be nice to have played or read at my funeral. I get inspiration and comfort from walking in the churchyard opposite my country house, imagining the lives lived. A writer friend told me he always uses a walk around a graveyard to find names for his characters. My favourite inscription on a headstone is the writer and comedian Spike Milligan's. It says *"I told you I was ill."*

This poem is for my son – the nicest man it has ever been my good fortune to know ...

Look for Me

Look for me in springtime,
Hear me in the cuckoo's call,
Let's share the bluebells and the daffodils
Like we've been apart, no time at all,
And when the darling buds of May
Are ready to appear,
Let's walk together, you and I,
I promise I'll be near.

Look for me in summertime,
When you hear the blackbird sing,
My caress is in the gentle breeze
My love is on the wing.
Let's sit together and watch the sea,
Walk on a beach, just you and me,
Let's gaze at the stars in the Milky Way,
I'll still be with you night and day.

Look for me when autumn comes,
When rusty leaves scrape the ground,
I'll still be there when flowers fade,
I'll always be around,
Even when the nights draw in
And darkness falls too soon,
Look for pictures in the fire,
I'll be there in the room.

Look for me when winter falls
And the birds have flown away,
When the trees are bare and black
And the skies are dark and grey.
When the wind and rain blow to and fro
And rattle your windows and door,
Try to remember the good times we had
And let's make plans for more.

flapjackpress.co.uk